SEVEN
TIMES

BE FREE LIVE FREE

D1173018

KEITH GRABILL

ISBN: 978-1939456-11-3
Library of Congress Control Number: 2013957864

All Scripture References from NIV unless otherwise noted. In addition, these translations were used: NLT, LB, NASV, NKJV, AMP, MSG

Design by Michael Malone

Published by Search for the Truth Publications
3275 Monroe Rd.
Midland, MI 48642
www.searchforthetruth.net

Printed in Grand Rapids, MI, USA

A HUGE THANK YOU

To my beautiful wife, Lacei, who is my best friend, closest confidant, and co-dreamer. You are my inspiration.

To Ethan, Eric, and Kayla who are the three most amazing, fun, and caring kids in the universe.

To my close friends, Ben Stoffel, Tarick Chaleby, Michael Malone, and Bruce Malone, who came alongside me during this book journey. I am indebted to you.

To my hero, Dean Grabill, who is also my Dad. I have been blessed out of my mind.

GOOD THINGS AHEAD

MISSING A FINGER

Recently, we took a missions team to the country of Haiti. Months before the trip, the team was told repeatedly to be careful in what they ate and drank. Obviously, we wanted to be a help while we were there and not be sidelined by sickness. Our team arrived safely and began an amazing week. During one of the first meals, one of the guys spilled spaghetti sauce on his hairy leg. Before any of the students, leaders, or even our nurse could stop him, he licked the sauce right off of his leg. Most of us thought it was disgusting. Some thought it was funny. But, it was our nurse who quickly said, "There's our first casualty." The nurse was right on. Within 48 hours, the bacteria did its thing. He was out of the game and sidelined (in the bathroom).

Sickness has a way of sidelining and stopping people. One of the most feared sicknesses and diseases ever known to man was leprosy. This disease caused skin sores, nerve damage, and muscle weakness. Although it had a long incubation period before the symptoms appeared, as the disease worsened, the prospect of a normal, healthy life went out the door.

Many people would hide their leprosy for as long as possible in hopes that something would happen. Maybe it would just go away. Maybe they would wake up the next day and it would be better. Unfortunately, this wouldn't happen. Leprosy hit, and it hit hard. It didn't matter your age, status in life, amount of money, or if you were godly or ungodly.

This disease didn't play fair.

Eventually, the ugly, nasty, painful lumps and skin sores would surface, and they would never get better—only worse. Think of leprosy as fire. As long as there was something to burn, the fire of leprosy was never satisfied.

Because leprosy attacked the peripheral nerves, its victims typically lost feeling, especially in their hands and feet. Often, people with leprosy would burn themselves while cooking since they could not feel the heat. In addition, because they gradually would lose the ability to feel pain, leprosy sufferers would get cuts, sores or blisters on their feet from wearing ill-fitting shoes or continuing to walk on injured or cut feet.

Mark it up as urban legend, but I have even heard that if you had leprosy, a rat could literally chew off part of your finger while you slept. The rat crawls away with a full belly, and you wake up with only one knuckle. Not cool.

Yet, one of the most heart-wrenching realities of leprosy occurred when the disease was discovered by those around you. You were ostracized by those you used to call friends and neighbors. In Europe during the Middle Ages, leprosy sufferers had to wear special clothing, ring bells to warn others that they were close, and even walk on a particular side of the road, depending on the direction of the wind.[1] Because of the shameful nature of leprosy, you were looked down on and sent away to leper colonies. This was a forgotten place where you were forced to live out your days away from the non-lepers. Suddenly, you were not important or valued. This was not a life anyone signed up for.

So, is this a book about leprosy of old? No way.

This is a book about a modern day leprosy which hits harder, is more destructive, and whose casualties are sky-rocketing. This is a book about the internal leprosy of pornography.

Do you know anyone with a skin disease they can't hide? What do you think life is like for them?

Would you say most people in your life attempt to hide their weaknesses or openly reveal them? Why do you think that is?

What comparisons or contrasts could be made between the skin disease of leprosy and pornography?

BE REAL

YOU ARE SAFE HERE

A recent news article described the trauma many surgical patients are experiencing. Thousands of times a year, items are left in a patient's body after surgery. As the flesh is sown up, forceps, clamps, other hardware, and most often cotton sponges are unknowingly left behind. Obviously, this oversight wreaks havoc on the body. Certain patients suffer for months and sometimes years before X-rays are performed to determine the reason for the illnesses and pain caused by foreign objects.[2] Maybe it's just me, but I would call that an unsuccessful surgical experience.

Our mind and soul, like our physical body, do not react well to negative foreign materal. When a person allows the entrance of pornography into his or her life, the infection begins. This internal leprosy of pornography is strikingly familiar to the external leprosy that was feared for so long. Leprosy of old had a debilitating toll on the person as it ate away at the outside flesh of the body. But the toll of internal leprosy is far worse, as it eats away at the inner heart, soul, and mind of a person.

While leprosy primarily affected the skin and the nerves outside the brain, the internal leprosy of pornography directly affects the inside of the brain, which influences one's soul, one's relationships, and one's future. In fact, pornography gradually creates an agonizing makeover of the brain. From the world of neuroscience, we learn that pornographic visual images both quickly imprint and alter the brain by triggering an instant, but lasting biochemical memory trail. "Brain scientists tell us that in 3/10 of a second a visual image passes from the eye through the brain, and whether or not one wants to, the brain is structurally changed and memories are created—we literally 'grow new brain' with each visual experience."[3] This brain makeover explains why the images are so tough to get rid of and so hard to then get away from.

So, what is pornography? It can be hard to define, but when it's seen you know it. A friend of mine simply defined it in this way:

Pornography is looking sexually at someone who is not your spouse.

Would you read that last sentence again? This definition is all-encompassing in that it includes every area the enemy uses to infect you.

Just as no one would wake up one morning with full-blown leprosy all over his or her body, nobody develops a full blown pornography addiction in one night. It begins slowly. You notice that person. You see that commercial. You watch that show. You do a search online, then another, then another. It's a process. But, inevitably, the symptoms of this internal leprosy will begin to appear.

This internal leprosy of pornography is, I believe, the biggest issue right now in our society. It's one of the least talked about, but the most destructive. This leprosy is already destroying marriages and families, and it's poised to destroy young people's futures. So many have been exposed. And, it's not just you. Countless numbers of men, women, and young people are suffering as they experience it eating away at their closeness with God, their friendships, their relationships, their current or future marriages, and the vision God has for their lives. The real-life effects surfacing in individuals, in relationships, and in marriages are brutal. And, the thought of what the homes, marriages, churches, and the state of young people will look like in ten years, if this leprosy is not dealt with, haunts me.

The individuals whose faces I see right now compel me to write this book. They entered a world so appealing at first, but now find themselves caught, trapped, and ashamed. The unfortunate part is that many of them haven't seen the long-term effects of this leprosy. Then, there are others I see. It's the faces of those who haven't yet been exposed to this leprosy—the kids, the teenagers, and adults who haven't yet given in to the temptation.

Whatever the cost, they must be protected.

This book is a book of safety, not fear. It's a book of promise, not condemnation. It won't be in your face, but it will serve to come alongside you in your journey, wherever you are. It's a book of reality and, at the same time, a book of hope. Deep down some of you know it's gone too far. The road from curiosity, to attraction, to distraction, to struggle, and maybe even to addiction has happened way too quickly.

You can justify pornography. *Hey, everyone else is doing this. Everyone else is watching this.* You can discount it as if it's not a big deal. *It's just one look. It's just for a few minutes.* And, you can refuse to accept the short and long-term damage. *This doesn't affect me. I can handle it.* But, reality says something completely different.

Something needs to change. I believe the time is now to proclaim God's ability to heal. Understand that this is not a self-help experience. A self-help book is about you and what you can do. Most have already discovered that this leprosy can't be beat by just trying harder or being smarter. This is a battle which requires the activity of God on your behalf. Thankfully, God unconditionally loves you and is all-powerful. This journey, then, is about what God wants to do and can do. You might think, *I just pray a prayer and the problem is over, right?* That's not exactly how it happens.

Only you can create the life environment where God can work.

Although this internal leprosy may have hit hard, you have the opportunity to experience the unlimited power of God. It's time for healing.

How would you define pornography?

What do you think this statement means: "Only you can create the life environment where God can work?"

On scale of 1-10, how satisfied are you with how your life is going right now? What holds you back from a higher level of satisfaction and peace?

BE REAL

STUCK IN NORMAL

Life was going extremely well for Naaman. Let's just say it. He was THE man. His family thought so. The king of his country definitely thought so. In fact, because Naaman had proven his courage on the battlefield, the king made him the commander of his entire army. Obviously, Naaman was a tough guy and a great leader. Thousands of men reported to him. Life was definitely going well for this guy. And, the future looked even better.

Except there was this one thing, one minor detail. This was the one area of his life that he would have given everything to keep a secret, and, he would have done anything to make it just go away. The Scriptures share Naaman's secret: "He was a valiant soldier, **but he had leprosy**" (2 Kings 5:1, emphasis added).

The man, the commander, the father had leprosy.

Likely, Naaman had attempted to cover up what was happening in his life for as long as possible.

But, the external symptoms had begun, and it couldn't be hidden any longer. His friends knew it. His family knew it. Even his boss knew it. There was no denying it. Something had to change or this leprosy was literally going to kill him. Although it's unclear how bad his case was at that moment, Naaman knew that leprosy didn't get better, only worse.

At some point, Naaman came to the end of his rope. He hit rock bottom and desperately went on a search for help. Wouldn't you? "Now bands from Aram had gone out and had taken captive a young girl from Israel, and she served Naaman's wife. She said to her mistress, 'If only my master would see the prophet who is in Samaria! He would cure him of his leprosy'"

(2 Kings 5:3). As this young girl began talking about a cure, I can just see a slight glimmer of hope appearing in Naaman's eyes. *You mean there's a possibility that I can be healed of my leprosy? Are you saying that I might not be stuck with this for the rest of my life?*

Naaman hears there is hope, and it's crazy what hope will do to a person. If there's hope for survival, a person will undergo unbelievable circumstances in order to stay alive. People have fought, scraped, and even drank their own urine because of the hope of rescue.

While Naaman didn't have to do all of that, he was about to face a challenge he had never faced on the battlefield. Thankfully, his king believed there was hope as well. The first words out of his mouth were, "By all means, go!" (2 Kings 5:5). So, he did. Naaman set out on a journey—a journey that would eventually transform his present and his future.

"So Naaman went with his horses and chariots and stopped at the door of Elisha's house" (2 Kings 5:9). This Elisha guy was not your normal dude. In that time period, Elisha was THE man of God. Naaman was definitely going to the right place. During the

Old Testament times, you rarely went directly to God. Instead, you found someone else who knew God.

Knock, knock, knock. Naaman shows up at the door of the man of God. This message is then given to Naaman: "Go, wash yourself seven times in the Jordan, and your flesh will be restored and you will be cleansed" (2 Kings 5:10). You would think that's great news. Just go wash in the Jordan, and no more leprosy, Naaman.

Well, the news wasn't as spectacular as you might think. Naaman wasn't exactly running to jump in the water. You see, the Jordan River is not exactly a hot tub or the hotel pool. It's nasty, believe me. Recently, I saw the Jordan River with my own eyes, and as I stood on the bank, I totally understood why Naaman wasn't a big fan. It was muddy, gross, and definitely not a place for an enjoyable swim. For someone of Naaman's fame and stature, washing in that particular river would be terribly embarrassing. Imagine the president of the United States being ordered to go for a dip in a stagnant swamp while the news media records the event for the world.

Naaman didn't like the prescription. The Scripture says, "Naaman went away angry and said, 'I thought that he would surely come out to me and stand and call on the name of the Lord his God, wave his hand over the spot and cure me of my leprosy. Are not Abana and Pharpar, the rivers of Damascus, better than any of the waters of Israel? Couldn't I wash in them and be cleansed?' So he turned and went off in a rage" (2 Kings 5:11-12).

In that moment, time stood still for Naaman. He was making a decision.

He knew this decision would radically affect his present and his future.

But in Naaman's mind, it just wasn't worth it.

Now, Naaman's leprosy was on the outside, but the reality is that millions have the leprosy of pornography on the inside. You see, there are great, talented, nice men and women in this world. Everything seems to be going well, except for one thing. They have leprosy. I'm talking about fathers and future fathers, mothers and future mothers, leaders and future leaders who are walking around with an internal leprosy.

This internal leprosy of pornography has the potential to destroy life after life after life. Unfortunately, this leprosy is not just a bad habit. We can beat those. It's not just a weakness. A self-help book can overcome that.

Every ounce of effort in the world won't beat this leprosy. More will-power or throwing away your computer or moving to a tribe in Africa will not win this fight. Although filters and accountability might help, the core issue is found in the heart and the mind. There's only ONE who can heal that, but you must decide if it's worth it.

In what ways could pornography hold you back?

Why do you think Naaman wasn't willing to do what he needed to do? Can you relate? When have you ever thought the words, "It's not worth it"?

Do you think there's hope for you?

How would your life be different without pornography?

WALKING AWAY

In traveling to other countries, I've discovered one of the most important phrases to learn is, "How much does it cost?" This phrase is said in countless different ways across the globe. Most people can learn how to ask it in a different language. My challenge has always been understanding what the local merchant actually says in reply. Usually, the reply is said quickly with a heavy accent. Although I've often acted like I understood what was said, many times I had no idea the kind of deal offered to me.

So, I've walked away from buying tissues, sunglasses, drinks, flip flops, sharp knives, and many other things. Was it because they cost too much? I'm not sure.

Maybe, I just didn't understand the great deal being offered. And, quite honestly, in that moment, it wasn't worth finding out. The travel tissues weren't worth me swallowing my pride and admitting that I couldn't understand a word the merchant had just said.

Now, let's go back to our friend Naaman. He was walking away from possible healing. In his mind, it wasn't worth it. The fight wasn't worth the embarrassment. I wonder what was going through Naaman's mind. *Maybe healing is not even possible. Why did I even come here? I can beat this on my own. It's bad, but it's not that bad. I can't believe that Elisha guy actually told me to wash in the Jordan River. How can I even be sure I would be healed? He could be wrong.*

It is easier to give in than to fight. It's easier to walk away than to move forward. And, it's definitely easier to go back to the prison we know, rather than venture into new territory and discover the freedom which is offered.

So many give in to a lifelong leprosy of pornography. Yet, they hate it. They're ashamed of it. And, they've given into believing this is the way life will be. Some think, *I can learn to live with this leprosy and manage it. I will not let it affect me or those around me. I definitely will not let it get any worse. And, I don't even know if healing and freedom are possible.* Sadly, they are deceived.

Naaman was content to go back home with leprosy rather than pursue healing.

Little did he know that contentment short of God's purposes destroys what could be.

Now, here's the crazy part: His leprosy was so horrible that he had left his own country on a search for healing. It's not like he traveled all the way next door. This was a journey, a long journey filled with hope and expectation. He had made the trip, but now he had decided to go limping back home.

So, what was he going back to? He would return to the same life he knew--a life of pain, a debilitating sickness, and a condition that would keep getting worse and worse. At some point, he wouldn't even be able to be around his wife and his kids. Speaking of them, I wonder what he was planning on telling his wife, his kids, and his king about what Elisha had said? He would have to tell them something. "Uhh, the man of God said to wash in the Jordan River seven times, but I didn't think it was worth it. So, I walked away." That probably wouldn't go well.

Naaman believed the lie that it wasn't worth it. The journey to freedom wasn't worth it. He had wanted what everyone wants–a quick fix. He even said in anger, "I thought that he would surely come out to me and stand and call on the name of the Lord his God, wave his hand over the spot and cure me of my leprosy" (2 Kings 5:11).

Naaman had his idea of how it should happen. *Just say something quick and my leprosy will be gone.* For many of you, the internal leprosy of pornography began with a click of a button. And, you wish it would go away with a click of a button. With one step you can get caught in quicksand. Although it would be nice if you could just step right out, it just doesn't work that way.

A life saving hand and a personal fight are a must to get out of the quicksand.

As Naaman was drowning in this quicksand of anger and pride, his servants threw him some life-saving advice. These wise servants came to him and said, "My father, if the prophet had told you to do some great thing, would you not have done it? How much

more, then, when he tells you, 'Wash and be cleansed!'"
(2 Kings 5:13).

Thank God for these people in his life. Thank God
there were people who cared enough to speak up.
Thank God there were people who saw the situation
clearly enough to shout out, "Hey Naaman, there's
hope. There's freedom. There's victory. IT'S WORTH
IT!"

He listened. And, here's my favorite part of
Naaman's journey. "He went down and dipped himself
in the Jordan seven times, as the man of God had told
him, and his flesh was restored and became clean like
that of a young boy" (2 Kings 5:14). Naaman had just
made the best decision of his life. This decision led to
his complete and lasting healing.

Will you make the best decision of your life? It's a
decision that will, without a doubt, affect you and those
around you for the rest of your life. It's a journey of
hope and freedom. If Naaman were here, he would
shout,

"IT'S WORTH IT!"

Is freedom worth whatever it takes to obtain it?

How does true freedom affect a person?

If you walk away without experiencing freedom from pornography, how will your life be different in 3 months, 1 year, 5 years?

If you choose to believe it's worth it and experience freedom from pornography, how will your life be different in 3 months, 1 year, 5 years?

BE REAL

THE
JUMP

Naaman's life was radically altered. One day he was headed for sure death by disease. There was no way around it. He had leprosy. Fair or not, he had leprosy. At this point, it didn't matter how he got it, where he got it, or how it began. He had leprosy. Then it happened–a radical healing, a total transformation. Now, leprosy had no hold on Naaman's life. The leprosy was a distant memory. And, he was going home a free man.

I wonder what would have happened if Naaman's response to Elisha's instructions would have been slightly different. Let's say Naaman didn't return to the Jordan River and just went on home, living life as he had been living. Would the leprosy have been healed?

No way.

The man of God told him to wash seven times in the Jordan. But, what if Naaman had only done one washing? What if he was really tired and could only manage four washings? What if, because of the busyness of his schedule, he only had time for six washings? That's a pretty high percentage, right? What would have happened? Nothing. He was instructed to wash seven times, not four, or two, or six. The number was seven.

Each of the seven washings was significant and absolutely vital for his complete healing.

Naaman's submission and obedience to this God-designed plan of seven washings brought about his cleansing.

How can you experience total freedom and healing from the destructive internal leprosy of pornography? Well, first understand that it's not a quick fix. This leprosy might have entered your life with a click of a button. Unfortunately, it doesn't leave with a simple click of the button. More than likely, freedom requires a process, a process of healing, a process of seven washings.

The rest of this book highlights the seven washings of the leprosy of pornography. There's good news. Victory and freedom are possible, and healing is yours to experience. My prayer is that even as you read these words the Lord is filling you with the reality of hope. Tomorrow will be different than today. Your past and even your present does not have to dictate your future. It didn't for Naaman, and this can be true for you as well.

Each of these seven washings works together to ensure victory. The first washing hinges on the second, and the third, and all the way to the seventh. If one isn't embraced, freedom will be harder to attain. Naaman washed seven times. And, each one was part of the process of healing. The good news is that through the process, he experienced healing. And, so will you!

Recently, I stood on the steps of a diving platform. I watched as some jumped off the high ledge and into the water below. Others went to the top, looked down, and decided against the plunge. Painfully and somewhat shamefully, they passed by me and climbed down the stairs with their heads down. It wasn't worth it, not that day.

As I climbed up the stairs and eventually stood on

the edge, I had to make a decision. Thankfully for me, I had friends right there with me encouraging me to jump. Below me, at the side of the pool stood my family. Their waves and big smiles were all I needed to jump off the platform. So, even though I can't swim extremely well, and I'm not a fan of high places, I swallowed my doubts and jumped (again, and again, and again).

We are cheering for you. You might have thought that freedom from pornography wasn't even possible. Right now, you might be wondering if the fight for freedom is even worth it. Please hear me. Those who care about you, your spouse, your future spouse, your kids, and your future kids are yelling as loud as they can, "It is worth it!" Even the God of the universe wants you to know, "It's worth it because you were born for freedom!"

Seven washings are awaiting you. Will you jump in? Will you jump into freedom?

I, _____, *want to live a life of freedom. The washings that bring me freedom will be the same washings that keep me free. I will not let my past dictate my future because the future God has for me is so amazing, I refuse to miss it.*

I, _____, *dedicate myself to pursue freedom and live free. This is not just for my future, but also for my family, friends, and future relationships.*

Date: _____

TAKE
ACTION

WASHING OF GRACE

WASHING OF THE WORD

WASHING OF PRAYER

WASHING OF ACCESS

WASHING OF CONFESSION

WASHING OF TRIGGERS

WASHING OF ACCOUNTABILITY

RESCUED

Several years ago, I heard about a group of Navy SEALs staging a covert operation. Their mission was to free American hostages from a building in a hostile country. The team flew in by helicopter, made their way to the compound, and stormed into the room where the hostages had been imprisoned for months. The room was dark and filthy. The hostages were discovered curled up in a corner paralyzed by fear.

The SEALs stood at the door and assured the hostages that they were Americans sent to rescue them. They asked the hostages to follow them, but they wouldn't. The hostages just sat on the floor and covered their eyes. The minds of the prisoners had been altered, and they didn't believe that their rescuers were truly Americans.

The SEALs didn't know what to do. They couldn't carry everyone out. All of a sudden, one of the SEALs had an idea. He took off his helmet, put his gun down, and curled up tightly next to the hostages. He put his arms around them. The SEAL was trying to show them that he was one of them. None of the prison guards would have done this.

He stayed there for awhile until one of the hostages looked at him and their eyes met. The Navy SEAL whispered that he was an American there to rescue them. "Will you follow us?" he asked. The hero stood up, and one of the hostages did the same, then another, until all of them were willing to go.

None of the hostages was physically and mentally able to leave on his own. It wasn't until someone came to him, right where he was. The Bible says, "This grace was given us in in Christ Jesus before the beginning of time, but it has now been revealed through the appearing of our Savior, Christ Jesus, who has destroyed death and has brought life and immortality to light through the Gospel" (2 Timothy 1:9-10).

Grace is Jesus Christ, God Himself, coming to where we are to rescue us. Jesus whispers to us and shouts to the world that He has come to bring life.

Through His grace, amazing rescue and freedom are now attainable.

Ephesians 2 gives a clear picture of our imprisoned nature before Christ. We are dead in sin, following the ways of the world, doing what we want when we feel like it, excluded, foreigners, without hope, far away, and separate from Christ. Clearly, this is not a good place to be, but this is the reality of every single person before the washing of grace in Christ Jesus.

Jesus came to your rescue by living the perfect life, dying the sacrificial death, and rising from the dead victorious over ALL of your sin. Now, your life, your past, your present, and your future can take on a complete makeover.

The same Scripture then paints the reality of life IN Christ. It describes this new life as being made alive in Christ, saved, raised up with Christ, seated with Christ in the heavenly realms, becoming God's workmanship, brought near to Him, being fellow citizens, and now given access to God Himself.

Through the washing of grace, you are not who you once were. You are a son or daughter of the King. Now, you have been given freedom, healing, and hope. This is who you are in Christ and the reality of what you are created to experience.

In this honest and humble moment, if you have never received this washing of the grace of salvation, would you let today be your day? Believe in Jesus, the One who displayed His love for you by dying on the cross to pay the penalty for your sins. Believe in God, the One who rose again victorious. Simply put, belief in Jesus is being fully persuaded that He is who He says He is and that He did what He said He would do. Receive this Jesus into your life and ask Him to be your King. You can call out to Him right now. Romans 10:13 says, "Everyone who calls on the name of the Lord will be saved."

If you are saved and washed by His grace, guess what? "There is now no condemnation for those who are in Christ Jesus" (Romans 8:1). Through the acceptance of the sacrifice of Jesus Christ, condemnation is replaced with freedom. How does that sound? There is no sentence of guilt. You are washed by grace.

Have you ever asked for forgiveness from someone but they keep bringing up what you have done? When someone wrongs us, it's hard for us to forget and let it go. But, in Christ, you have been forgiven and are free from condemnation. That is grace. And as a believer in Jesus Christ, you are now forgiven and secure.

Grace is the first washing away of the internal leprosy of pornography. It's the supernatural work of God we never deserved through our works and could never repay by our works. Grace is His favor on us that gives us undeserved forgiveness and an unimaginable new future.

Have you personally received the Salvation of Jesus Christ? If not, let this written prayer guide you:

Lord Jesus, I acknowledge that You and You alone are the King of this universe. Because of my sin and unbelief, I have fallen short. I need You. Please forgive me of all my many sins against You. Wash me in your forgiveness and grace. I believe that through Your death and resurrection my Salvation is now possible. Now, I ask you to be the King of my life. My life is no longer about me, but it is about you and for you. Thank you for saving me. Thank you for washing me in Your grace.

WASHING OF GRACE

WASHING OF
THE WORD
WASHING OF
PRAYER
WASHING
OF ACCESS
WASHING OF
CONFESSION
WASHING OF
TRIGGERS
WASHING OF
ACCOUNTABILITY

MY LICENSE

Do you remember looking forward to finally receiving your driver's license? You grow up thinking, *One day, I will have freedom.* After the seemingly endless wait, the day arrives. You barely miss the pedestrian, squeak by on the written test, and are miraculously presented with your first driver's license. Now, according to your state government, you are free to drive the car of your dreams. Well, my first car hadn't exactly been in my dreams. In fact, it wasn't even my car. It was my parent's car. Sure, it looked like an old lady's car, but I had a license to drive it. Thankfully, I had that license with me when a policeman asked for it within the first two weeks. Ouch!

Just like many receive a license to drive, some think God's grace is a license to sin: *Hey, I'm saved. God has forgiven me of all my sins. I'm good now. Grace is my get out of jail free card. Let the fun begin.* One young man wrote this: "God knew His sons and daughters would engage in sin. So, I'm not gonna let something I occasionally enjoy condemn me. I know the power of what God did. I know how much He loves me. And, no matter what I do He will never leave my side."

With his opinion in mind, take a look at this Scripture: "For certain men whose condemnation was written about long ago have secretly slipped in among you. They are godless men, who change the grace of our God into a license for immorality and deny Jesus Christ our only Sovereign and Lord" (Jude 4).

Unfortunately, there can be a great misunderstanding of the purpose and power of God's grace. Some think it's a license to sin and then ask the wrong questions. The question, "How far is too far?" is the wrong question. The question, "Is grace a license to sin?" is also the wrong question. Paul the apostle said,

"What shall we say, then? Shall we go on sinning so that grace may increase? By no means! We died to sin; how can we live in it any longer?" (Romans 6:1-2)

Grace is not a free license to sin–not even close. By God's grace you are dead to sin. By God's grace you are no longer a slave to sin. This is why it's so important for an unbeliever connected to pornography to experience the washing of grace. Confess your sins and believe on Jesus.

Equally important is the need for believers in Jesus, who have opened themselves to the leprosy of porn, to experience the washing of grace. This washing is a clearer understanding of the dynamic force of grace available to us.

By the washing of God's grace, "You have been set free from sin" (Romans 6:18). You are completely set free. Contrary to what many think, grace is not a license to sin.

Grace is the license to live!

"For we know that our old self was crucified with him so that the body of sin might be done away with, that we should no longer be slaves to sin—because anyone who has died has been freed from sin" (Romans

6:6-7).

Freedom from sin and the chains of pornography may sound almost too good to be true. It doesn't sound normal or even possible. Truly, it sounds supernatural. And, that is precisely the reality of grace. It's God's supernatural gift of power and freedom in your life through the work of Jesus Christ.

This was transformational in my own life. Through the washing of grace, I realized I am no longer a slave to sin. So, when temptation comes my way (and it does), no longer do I have to give in. I am free.

I have been given the license to live free.

Temptation and sin have no legitimate hold on us any longer. Romans 6 declares, "Sin shall not be your master, because you are not under law, but under grace" (Romans 6:14). A washing of grace transforms how you think. You and I are free. No longer do you have to sin.

In addition, the more I am washed with the understanding of His grace, the more I don't want to sin. Why? It's simple. I want to please my Savior, Jesus Christ, "who saved me and called me to live a holy life"

(2 Timothy 1:9). His grace has given you a license to live a free life!

Read this statement from someone washed in God's grace: "I don't resist sin because I'm scared of God's judgment or losing my salvation. I resist sin because I love God and His nature is inside of me. I don't serve God because I'm scared of what will happen if I don't, or because I want to get some blessing. I serve Him because my spirit has been awakened to Him and my spirit is full of His passion, love, and purpose."[4]

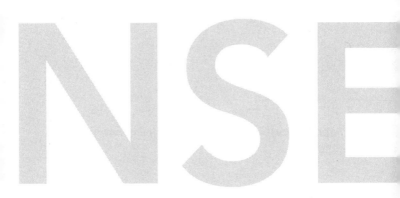

In the past, what effect do you think involvement with pornography had on your relationship with God, family, friends, and your self-esteem?

Think about the last time you faced temptation. How did you respond? Why did you respond in this way?

Through the washing of grace, how can you now respond to temptations?

From this chapter, how would you define grace?

Read Romans 6. How does the reality of grace change the way you think?

WASHING OF GRACE

WASHING OF
THE WORD
WASHING OF
PRAYER
WASHING
OF ACCESS
WASHING OF
CONFESSION
WASHING OF
TRIGGERS
WASHING OF
ACCOUNTABILITY

UN-CHAINED

It was a hot summer day right after seventh grade ended. Finally classes were over, and I could start earning some money by mowing yards. On one infamous day I was mowing a yard close to my middle school. The owner's dog was chained to a stake right in the middle of the yard I was mowing. At some point, I knew I would be forced to turn the lawnmower off to reposition the dog, the chain, and the stake. But, what seventh grader has time to do all of that?

Being in a hurry, I wanted to get as close as possible to the chain lying in the yard before having to move it. Closer and closer I mowed until I heard a nasty noise. The lawnmower blade had caught the dog chain. Unbeknownst to him, the nice doggie was about to have a traumatic experience. As soon as the chain caught, the unsuspecting dog was instantly catapulted off it's feet and dragged mercilessly toward the rotating blade. Scared to death, I let go of the lever and waited for the bloodbath. Right when the dog made it to the blade, the blade came to a stop. The dog survived with a concussion and a lifetime dose of nightmares. I, however, barely survived the extremely angry dog owner.

On that summer day, this particular dog had no chance of escaping his life-threatening experience. It was chained to the stake. Most likely, you or someone you know is chained to a stake as well–the addiction of pornography. You might even have told yourself some messages like these: *I'm a sinner, I'm going to sin, I'm an imperfect person, the pull is too much, I can't get away from this, I'm going to fail again, and again, and again.* As long as you tell yourself these things and believe that victory is impossible, you will not experience freedom.

When you embrace the apparent limitations, you will always be confined by them.

But, then you hear about GRACE! You begin to

be washed with the understanding of salvation and the freedom from condemnation in Christ. Oh, and don't forget the supernatural license to live free.

There's something else you need to understand about the grace of Jesus Christ. It's empowerment. You see, grace is the dynamic force that makes the impossible, possible. Through the washing of grace, you are empowered to go beyond what's natural or considered normal.

The book of Romans says, "Sin shall not have dominion over you, for you are not under law but under grace" (6:14). Through this empowerment of grace, you are no longer chained to sin, addictions, and strongholds. Sin was too powerful, but not anymore. Before the washing of grace, you stood no chance. Now, the chain is gone.

"Since we are receiving a Kingdom that cannot be shaken, let us have grace, by which we may serve God acceptably" (Hebrews 12:28). God's grace gives you the ability to go beyond the previous limits. You might have heard people say, "You will sin at some point and you will fall down eventually." This is not Scriptural. Grace empowers you to live free of the limits of sin and the chain of pornography now and in the future.

Each believer does, of course, have the capability to sin. However, this is a choice of the mind and not an obligation to the flesh.

In other words, the grace of Jesus Christ does not remove the temptation to sin or your choice to sin. This grace does, though, give you all the power you need to live in freedom from the sin of pornography. Don't think of it as an alien abduction where you are unknowingly and helplessly whisked away from temptation by odd looking martians, never to return. You still have a free will. You still live on this earth. But, you are not a chained slave to sin any longer. As you create the life environment where God can work, you will experience the empowerment of His grace.

One of my all-time favorite Scriptures is 2 Peter 1:3-4. "His divine power has given us everything we need for a life of godliness through our knowledge of him who called us by his own glory and goodness. Through these he has given us his very great and precious promises, so that through them you may participate in the divine nature and escape the corruption in the world caused by evil desires." Read it again. Notice these words: "power," "everything," "escape."

The washing of grace empowers us to live beyond

the limits. There is no sin too strong, no leprosy too advanced, no addiction too powerful that you can't overcome! Romans 12:2 says, "Don't copy the behavior and customs of this world, but let God transform you into a new person by changing the way you think. Then you will learn to know God's will for you, which is good and pleasing and perfect" (NLT). It's a washing–a continual washing of the reality of God's grace. The more you understand His grace the less you will want to sin, the more you will want to please God, the more secure you will feel in God, and the more empowered you will live.

The impossible is now possible.

How would you describe to someone else what it feels like to be chained to pornography or another life-controlling issue?

How would you define the washing of grace?

Is it possible to not sin? Give several reasons for why you answered this way.

Read 2 Peter 1:3-11. What promises jump out at you from this passage?

WASHING OF
GRACE
WASHING OF
THE WORD
WASHING OF
PRAYER
WASHING
OF ACCESS
WASHING OF
CONFESSION
WASHING OF
TRIGGERS
WASHING OF
ACCOUNTABILITY

WINNING

It's hard to picture Jesus having a hard time with temptation. Think about it. God, in His power, could flick the enemy away like a piece of granola left on His sleeve. The scenario, though, was a bit different when Jesus came to the earth. Although He was still fully God, He also became fully man. And, even though he lived a completely pure life, he was, in fact, bombarded with temptation in every way, just as we are.

In Matthew 4, we are given a glimpse into the onslaught of temptation Jesus experienced (at least that day's worth). The enemy was coming at him hardcore, something you and I can relate to. But Jesus withstood and won. So, how did He win against temptation? He used the Word of God. At every turn of temptation,

Jesus fought back with Scripture. And, every time, He won, every time. Catch that:

He won every time.

No team wins every time. Even the best teams get upset occasionally. Many of you can probably better relate to the teams I played on. We lost, a lot. From time to time, maybe we would win. Usually, we were as surprised as the other team that we actually had won. The leprosy of pornography can feel like that. Sure, there's a good day from time to time. But, more often than not, it's defeat rather than victory. The thought of winning every time against this enemy seems unattainable.

Paul said in Ephesians 6:13, "To put on the full armor of God, so that when the day of evil comes, you may be able to stand your ground." All of the armor listed in that particular passage are vital to standing strong. And, every part of the armor is defensive—all except one. The sword of the Spirit is unique to the others in that it is an offensive weapon. God has given you this sword of the Spirit to fight with. Can you guess what this weapon is? It's the Word of God. It's the offensive weapon Jesus used to win. And, thankfully, He has given it to you, so you can fight against the leprosy of pornography.

However, the Word of God doesn't exist exclusively for you to have something to fight with. The Word of God is Truth, which is something everyone is starving for in the fight against leprosy. You see, the leprosy of pornography is one big deception. It deceives you into believing those images will bring satisfaction and will meet your needs. The reality is that pornography is leprosy and it is utterly unable to bring joy, happiness, and relational intimacy into your life. It never has and never will. That's the deception. It's clearly a lie from the enemy. Once a person steps away from the situation, the fog clears, and the reality hits. The leprosy of pornography is not your friend. Beyond just being a counterfeit, this leprous deception is actually your worst nightmare.

Isn't it unbelievable how temptation can mess with your mind? Or, more honestly, isn't it unbelievable how people can deceive themselves into believing a known lie? Your mind is powerful, but it can only hold one thought at a time. So, if your mind is consumed with a deceptive thought, there is no room for the truth. It's before this tempting moment, in this tempting moment, and after this tempting moment that your mind must be washed with the truth of God's Word.

Ephesians 5 says, "Christ loved the church. He gave up his life for her to make her holy and clean, **washed by the cleansing of God's word.** He did this to present her to himself as a glorious church without a spot or wrinkle or any other blemish. Instead, she will be holy and without fault" (vv. 25-27, NLT, emphasis added).

God's Word has a way of washing away the deception of the enemy from your mind. For many of you, the enemy has had free reign over your minds. When you choose for your mind to be washed with the Word, transformation takes place. Suddenly, lies are washed with God's Word. Deception is washed with Truth.

Remember, your mind can only hold one thought at a time. In a moment of temptation, that individual thought either aligns with God's Word of Truth or it doesn't. This is why you are instructed to take captive every thought to make it obedient to Christ.

In Jesus' battle against temptation, He filled His mind with the Word of God. Then, He spoke out the very words of God. In one instance, the enemy tried to deceive Jesus by offering the kingdoms of the world.

All of them would supposedly be given to Jesus if He would just bow down to Satan. Jesus fought back with the Word of God: "Away from me, Satan! For it is written: Worship the Lord your God, and serve him only" (Matthew 4:10).

Then, it happened. The devil left him. When faced with the temptation of pornography, wash your mind with the reality of the Word of God by reading it. Then, speak it out. Wash your mind with His Truth: *I am dead to sin. I have been set free from sin. Sin is no longer my master because of His grace. God is faithful. He will not let me be tempted beyond what I am able to bear. Right now, through His grace, His Word, and the washings to come, I am free from this leprosy!*

It is crucial that your mind is washed with the truth of God's Word—again, and again, and again. Frequent exposure to the truth of God's Word actually has the power to recalibrate your thought patterns. This leprosy may be tough, but it is no match for the power of God's Truth.

BE REAL

What is the deception of pornography?

When do you feel the most tempted?

What precedes the temptation to engage in pornography (i.e. anger, fatigue, loneliness, stress, etc.)?

How did Jesus fight when temptation came His way?

Read Matthew 4:1-11. What scriptures can help YOU win battles?

WASHING OF
GRACE
**WASHING OF
THE WORD**
WASHING OF
PRAYER
WASHING
OF ACCESS
WASHING OF
CONFESSION
WASHING OF
TRIGGERS
WASHING OF
ACCOUNTABILITY

SWORD FIGHTING

One of the most memorable things I saw as a child was Niagara Falls. Before my eyes even saw the water, I could hear its roar. To think that people have attempted to walk over it or jump into it unprotected blows my mind. One daredevil, named Blondin, actually carried his manager on his back while he walked on the tightrope across the falls. Crazy!

The power of the Falls is breathtaking. You can hear it and feel it. The sheer force and energy of the water falling over the edge produces massive amounts of power. In the battle against the leprosy of pornography, know that the Word of God is even more powerful. It has the potential to wash our minds with the very words which flow from the mouth of God. Day after day, it has the potential to wash, cleanse, and reprogram our thinking.

The following Scriptures are a gift from God to you. They are powerful for the washing of your mind. Fill your mind with them. Speak them out. Each verse pours freedom into your life. This chapter is not designed for a one time reading. Instead, it is designed to provide a continual washing of your mind with the powerful flow of God's Word.

Right now, you can begin to wash, fight, and win with these promises.

"How can a young man keep his way pure? By living according to your word. I seek you with all my heart; do not let me stray from your commands. I have hidden your word in my heart that I might not sin against you. Praise be to you, O Lord; teach me your decrees. With my lips I recount all the laws that come from your mouth. I rejoice in following your statutes as one rejoices in great riches. I meditate on your precepts and consider your ways. I delight in your decrees; I will not neglect your word." (Psalm 119:11-16)

"No, despite all these things, overwhelming victory is mine through Christ, who loves me." (Romans 8:37, NLT)

"No test or temptation that comes my way is beyond the course of what others have had to face. All I need to remember is that God will never let me down; He'll never let me be pushed past my limit; He'll always be there to help me come through it." (1 Corinthians 10:13, MSG)

"I am with you; that is all you need. My power shows up best in weak people." (2 Corinthians 12:9, LB)

"For everyone born of God overcomes the world. This is the victory that has overcome the world, even our faith." (1 John 5:4, NAS)

"Submit yourselves, then, to God. Resist the devil, and he will flee from you." (James 4:7)

"The God of peace will soon crush Satan under my feet!" (Romans 16:20, LB)

"You are from God, little children, and have overcome them; because greater is He who is in you than he who is in the world." (1 John 4:4, NASV)

"Happy is the man who doesn't give in and do wrong when he is tempted, for afterwards he will get as his reward the crown of life that God has promised those who love Him." (James 1:12, LB)

"And I pray that Christ will be more and more

at home in your hearts as you trust in Him. May your roots go down deep into the soil of God's marvelous love. And may you have the power to understand, as all God's people should, how wide, how long, how high, and how deep His love really is." (Ephesians 3:17-18, LB)

"And I am convinced and sure of this very thing, that He who began a good work in me will continue until the day of Jesus Christ [right up to the time of His return], developing [that good work] and perfecting and bringing it to full completion in me." (Philippians 1:6, AMP)

"I cried out, 'I'm slipping!' and Your unfailing love, O LORD, supported me." (Psalms 94:18, NLT)

"And now, all glory to God, who is able to keep me from stumbling, and who will bring me into His glorious presence innocent of sin and with great joy." (Jude 24, NLT)

"The angel of the Lord encamps around those who fear Him, and He delivers them." (Psalm 34:7)

"For You are my hiding place; You protect me from trouble. You surround me with songs of victory." (Psalm 32:7, NLT)

"Have you never heard or understood? Don't you

know that the LORD is the everlasting God, the Creator of all the earth? He never grows faint or weary. No one can measure the depths of His understanding. He gives power to those who are tired and worn out; He offers strength to the weak. Even youths will become exhausted, and young men will give up. But those who wait on the LORD will find new strength. They will fly high on wings like eagles. They will run and not grow weary. They will walk and not faint." (Isaiah 40:28-31, NLT)

"I must be prepared. I am up against far more than I can handle on my own. I will take all the help I can get, every weapon God has issued, so that when it's all over but the shouting I'll still be on my feet." (Ephesians 6:13, MSG)

"I will not fear, for You are with me. I will not be anxiously looking about, for You are my God. You will strengthen me, surely You will help me. Surely You will uphold me with Your right hand of righteousness." (Isaiah 41:10, NASB)

"For God is at work in me, helping me to want to obey Him, and then helping me do what He wants." (Philippians 2:13, LB)

"Now I am free from the power of sin and I am a love-servant of the Lord's. His benefits to me are holiness and everlasting life." (Romans 6:22, LB)

"And I am convinced that nothing can ever separate me from His love. Death can't, and life can't. The angels can't, and the demons can't. My fears for today, or worries about tomorrow, and even the powers of hell can't keep God's love away. Whether I am high above the sky or in the deepest ocean, nothing in all creation will ever be able to separate me from the love of God that is revealed in Christ Jesus my Lord." (Romans 8:38-39, NLT)

The leprosy of pornography has a way of programming your mind.

It's truly like a computer virus which seeks to replicate itself again and again as it executes code and writes into the memory. Over time, the leprosy of pornography multiplies and affects the function of the mind. Many experience a drastic change in their view of themselves and of the opposite sex.

One friend described this phenomenon perfectly when he said, "My mind needs to be reprogrammed." The washing of the Word of God over your mind literally has the power to reprogram your thinking. Through continual washing, the way you view yourself, others, and life comes into alignment with the reality of God's Word. Wash your mind with the Word of God, and wash often.

What do you honestly believe is more powerful: The Word of God or the temptation you face?

Which of the Scriptures from this chapter stand out to you?

How could you activate the Word of God during the day? (i.e. read the Scripture at breakfast, memorize at lunchtime, journal your thoughts from the Word, etc...)

BE REAL

WASHING OF
GRACE
WASHING OF
THE WORD
WASHING OF
PRAYER
WASHING
OF ACCESS
WASHING OF
CONFESSION
WASHING OF
TRIGGERS
WASHING OF
ACCOUNTABILITY

GUARANTEED
GUARANTEED
GUARANTEED
GUARANTEED

Have you ever been dead tired? Sure, I have been tired many times, but then there are those times when all you want to do is curl up and go comatose for awhile. Youth camp was normally one of those times, especially when I had to drive home. One year, I had stayed up way too late for way too many nights making sure everyone else was sleeping, which was totally not fair. On Friday, as we packed up the luggage into the back of my truck, I knew it was going to be a rough ride home. I rolled the windows down, yelled, stuck my head out the window, and played drums on the steering wheel, just to keep my eyelids from shutting. I was dead tired.

One night, the disciples couldn't stay awake either. Unfortunately for them, it was THE night they needed to stay awake. Jesus was in the garden of Gethsemane preparing to be arrested and offer Himself as the sacrifice for sins. He asked the disciples to pray. This was THE night. But, they fell asleep. He woke them up. They fell asleep again. Then, Jesus gave them these life-saving words: "Watch and pray so that you will not fall into temptation. The spirit is willing, but the body is weak" (Matthew 26:41).

There's no doubt the disciples were exhausted. But, sleep was not what they needed. In a matter of minutes, temptation was coming. It would literally be felt as it came full force toward them.

Prayer was the life preserver Jesus was offering.

Jesus knew the temptation was on the way, but in that moment, the disciples couldn't see it coming. So, they slept.

Prayer is one of the fundamental ways the leprosy of pornography is washed away. Jesus taught us to pray in Matthew 6. Right in the middle of this prayer model are the words, "Lead us not into temptation" (v. 13).

This is powerful. Many people pray that they will not give in to the temptation. Jesus didn't begin there. He taught us to pray before the temptation even comes our way. *God, I pray that I will not even be tempted today. God, I pray that my heart will be so focused on you that I will not even notice the temptation.*

Have you always assumed temptation would be a part of your day? Here's a revolutionary idea straight from Jesus. Pray before the temptation arrives that it won't arrive! Prayers like this put you on alert. Now, you are not blindly walking into temptation. On the contrary, you are already calling out to God for His help, even before the temptation shows up.

Now, let's be real. This leprosy is a fight you won't win by yourself. You need healing and freedom that you can't obtain on your own. The washing of prayer is showing your all-out dependence on Jesus Christ. King David got it. In Psalm 18, he prayerfully called out to his rock, fortress, deliverer, refuge, shield, and salvation. Right in the middle of temptation, prayer is your way of escape.

There aren't many guarantees in life. Everything breaks, wears out, or loses its effectiveness—except prayer. I love the guarantee of Galatians 5:16: "Walk in the Spirit and you will not fulfill the lusts (the craving, desire for the forbidden) of the flesh" (NKJV). What a guarantee!

When a person receives salvation, the Spirit of God moves in. This Spirit of God is completely perfect and holy in every way. Through worship and prayer, you can actually tune in to the desires (what He wants) and the empowerment (what He can do) of the Spirit of God. A radio's output is simply static until you tune into the right station. Before and during a moment of temptation, tune in to the Spirit of God, and the pull of temptation will lose it's strength, guaranteed.

Here is one last tip about the washing of prayer. Pray before temptation, during temptation, and **AFTER** temptation. In prayer, thank God for His strength, His freedom, and His deliverance from another temptation.

Here's a GREAT way to pray BEFORE the tempation comes:

God, I need you today. Even before temptation comes my way, I humbly call out to you. Please help me to remain so focused on You that I will not even notice temptations the enemy throws my way. Protect me from his attacks as I depend completely on You. I want to thank you in advance for the strength and power you have already given me to win over temptation. Through You, I walk in victory. Amen.

WASHING OF
GRACE
WASHING OF
THE WORD
WASHING OF
PRAYER
WASHING
OF ACCESS
WASHING OF
CONFESSION
WASHING OF
TRIGGERS
WASHING OF
ACCOUNTABILITY

EXTREME

"Too much access!" This was the first thing a friend told me as he was struggling with this leprosy. Access was the problem. So easy. So accessible. TOO accessible. I wholeheartedly agree.

Several decades ago, it wasn't as accessible. Sure, you could find pornography, but it was a lot harder. A discarded magazine might be found in an alley, or it could be purchased from certain stores. Today, that's not the case. It's on the computer, TV, game systems, iPods, iPads, and phones. In his or her pocket, a person can carry instant access to anything the flesh wants to see. In the living room, it's there. In the privacy of the bedroom, it's there. Access.

Let's be honest. This accessibility is not an accident. 1 Peter 5:8 says, "Your enemy the devil prowls around like a roaring lion looking for someone to devour." In the day we live in, there is a lot of devouring going on. Men and women of all ages are being targeted. To add injury to insult, we are the ones who purchase the very tools for self-destruction and future derailment.

There must be a washing of the access. You might think, *I have to have my computer, my phone, and my game system.* This, my friends, is one of the lies our society believes. It's as if owning these devices is our right and our entitlement. Some even wonder how they can live without access to the internet at any given moment.

However, the internal leprosy of pornography calls for radical actions. If the access you keep giving into is the computer, remove it from your room or ask your family or friends to lock it down. If the access is the phone, take the internet off of it. *But, this is extreme!* Yes. So is the leprous destruction of pornography.

One young man who craved freedom from the leprosy wrote these words:

> *"One day I 'accidentally' dropped my PSP off a ledge. Of course, I didn't want to really break it. It's just what I thought I should do because I'm a Christian. And, this is wrong. The only thing that broke was the back case that houses where to put the game in. The screen was fine, which*

meant more searching. My parents bought me a new PSP that Christmas, which was not good. Also this summer, I found out that I could watch inappropriate videos on my brother's iPod touch. I would do it when he wasn't home, and I was home alone. My parents noticed that I was using his iPod more, so for Christmas I got a new iPod touch. The next best thing was now on my iPod–porn videos. This continued into my 12th grade year.

It was never an everyday thing, but mostly an every other week kind of thing. And the other weeks, I would actually try to be a Christian. But, the thoughts always came back when I was home alone. Then, in the spring of my 12th grade year, I was watching some videos on my iPod. I went outside to clean my car. I just needed to get out of my house because I was home alone again. So, as I'm cleaning my car, I decided I had had enough of that stinkin iPod and what I could look at. So, I unplugged it from my headphones and looked at it over the water bucket the soap was in. And, I just dropped it in there. Then, I picked it out of there and started to spray in the headphone jack to try to break it more internally. I realized the screen still looked kinda good, so I just spiked it on the ground three different times. The screen cracked and it didn't turn on. I felt a little bit of relief."

This extreme leprosy calls for extreme measures.

Washing the access is vital for victory. But, just like all of the other washings, this is just one of several vital washings. As you have just read, simply taking away a device does not change the heart or the addiction. However, washing the access enables you to get further and further from the temptation. While you are experiencing the washing of grace, the Word, and prayer, begin to wash the access as well.

Walking into an all-you-can-eat buffet is not wise for the person who struggles with obesity. Walking into a bar is not wise for the person who struggles with alcoholism. Walking around with access to pornography is a recipe for destruction for anyone who struggles with this internal leprosy. Let the washing begin.

Do you think it's by accident that pornographic images are so accessible in today's world?

Who are the victims in this industry?

What are your main points of ACCESS to pornography?

How important is it to you that your ACCESS be washed? What will you do about it?

BE REAL

WASHING OF
GRACE
WASHING OF
THE WORD
WASHING OF
PRAYER
WASHING
OF ACCESS
WASHING OF
CONFESSION
WASHING OF
TRIGGERS
WASHING OF
ACCOUNTABILITY

SECRECY

There are certain times when I'm beyond thankful that God created me to be a guy. The birth of my children was one of them. My wife and I are blessed with three amazing kids. What a joy it is to be called Daddy! However, from observation, I know the actual birth of the child is extremely painful. As a kid, my dad used to say while he was disciplining me that it hurt him as much as it hurt me. I didn't even try to use that line when my wife was giving birth to our kids. It wouldn't have been a good idea. It's beyond my comprehension what that intense pain must feel like. But, as soon the baby is born, there's an overwhelming joy. Was the pain of childbirth forgotten? Not entirely. But the joy of birth far outweighs the pain of birth. That's what I'm told anyway.

Confession has similarities to childbirth. There comes a time when it has to be done. Quite possibly for you, it's past due. How long have you been carrying this secret? Over time, it gets bigger and bigger. It could be pride or the foreseeable pain that keeps you from confessing to someone: *What will they think? Will they look down on me? Will they think less of me? Will I be labeled as one of "those" people? Will my reputation or my position take a hit?* In reality, we don't want people to see us as we might see ourselves. But, listen to this advice I heard somewhere along the journey:

"You better tell on your sin. If not, it will tell on you."

Let me be honest. The washing of confession will be one of the most difficult parts of this healing process. Up to this point, you may have been tracking well with each washing. The concepts make sense, and you have seen progress "on your own." But, this one is different. Truly, confession is always painful, at first— whether it's being caught as a little kid who stole candy or explaining to your loved ones, spouse, or future spouse about your leprosy of pornography. Even Job in the Old Testament echoed this sentiment when he said, "How painful are honest words!" (Job 6:25).

Through the washing of confession, though, you can experience the joy of victory. Someone wrote of his internal battle against confession: "The longer I kept my secret, the more I believed I could never share it. The longer I kept silent, the darker and stronger my sin grew. The longer I kept silent, the more convinced I became that I would just have to live the rest of my life with this."[5]

The washing of confession is powerful. James 5:16 says, "Therefore, confess (to acknowledge openly and joyfully) your sins to each other and pray for each other so that you may be healed." When healing is on the horizon, confession can actually bring joy. Most people have experienced the weight of guilt literally lift off their shoulders at some time during their lives when they have confessed.

Through confession, you are admitting that you don't have it all together. So, initially, this washing is a difficult and humbling experience. However, "God gives grace to the humble" (James 4:6). Through confession, grace (God's empowerment) and healing are given access to your life. Even though you might try to convince yourself that you can beat this leprosy, that you can skip this washing, and that no one else needs to know, the reality is that healing comes through confession. Gone are the days of keeping your struggle a secret. That never worked anyway.

Yes, confession is hard. Yes, you will have to fight like crazy to actually open your mouth and verbalize your struggle to someone. But, freedom is worth fighting for. Understand the washing of confession takes the secret out of the secret sin. Secrecy is the very thing that makes pornography so attractive. No one else knows. This is private. But the very part which made it attractive is actually the very part that makes it so destructive. As you might be experiencing, the leprosy of pornography gets worse and worse.

For a time, no one seems to even notice—except you, except God. However, there will come a time when the secret will no longer be a secret. There will come a time when the symptoms of leprosy will become clearly visible to those around you.

Either tell on the leprosy now or it will tell on you later.

The washing of confession is vital to your healing

and restoration. "Whoever conceals their sins does not prosper, but the one who confesses and renounces them finds mercy" (Proverbs 28:13).

Confession. The word can strike fear into the hearts of many. This washing might even appear to be the most difficult one in this book. Leave this one out, and freedom will be hard to come by. The washing of confession is one of the most powerful and needed of all the seven washings.

What makes confession so difficult for people?

What makes confession difficult for you? What has held you back from confessing to someone?

Do you believe this leprosy can be beat without confession? Why or why not?

Read Psalm 32:1-5, James 5:16, and 1 John 1:9. What secrets does the Bible share about confession?

WASHING OF
GRACE
WASHING OF
THE WORD
WASHING OF
PRAYER
WASHING
OF ACCESS
**WASHING OF
CONFESSION**
WASHING OF
TRIGGERS
WASHING OF
ACCOUNTABILITY

TEAM

The washing of confession might seem daunting. You may still be thinking, *Who do I talk with? Who will understand what I'm going through? Will I see compassion in their eyes or a look of disdain?* It's true that who you confess to is very important. Standing up on your lunch table at school or at work probably isn't the best idea. But remember that God is more interested in your freedom and future than even you are. I'm convinced He will provide someone in your life you can speak with. Ask the Lord for wisdom. Take the opportunity.

Now, let me share with you three parts of confession. The first part is the **Initial Confession**. Most people have not stepped through this one because it can be the most painful and seemingly shameful. Recently, a young man prayed, "God, if Keith walks over here, I will tell him." Thankfully, I "happened" to walk right over to him right after he prayed this prayer.

God Himself is calling you to confession, and He will give you the opportunities to do so. Still, you will need to pray for those moments, and when they come, be obedient to open your mouth. When this young man saw me walk up, his head dropped. Very quietly, in obedience to his prayer, he opened up and shared his leprosy of pornography. It's a monumental moment when a person finally confesses the secrets of his or her life. Although painful, the initial confession opens your heart and life to healing.

The second part is a **Continual Confession**. It's not a once and done. Once the confession is out there, the washing begins. The importance of this part of confession is huge. As you are experiencing, the freedom from this struggle is normally not won through a one time prayer. It's a process. If the struggle doesn't go away in a day, the confession must not go away either. Every time you share your struggle with someone you trust, you are putting the enemy on notice. This leprosy will be beat! You, through the grace and power of Jesus Christ, will win!

The third part of confession is the **Confession**

of Victory. This is the fun one. And, it is just as important as the Initial and Continual Confession. As you embrace the seven washings in this book, you are going to experience victory. Victory must be shared and declared.

When you are victorious for three days, one week, two months, or two years, tell someone. The book of Revelation says, "They overcame him [the enemy] by the blood of the Lamb and by the word of their testimony . . ." (12:11). Normally, we think of a testimony as what you give in front of the judge in court. You testify of the whole truth out loud as you sit in the witness stand. You testify to what you have seen, heard, and experienced.

In the path to victory over this struggle, your testimony is powerful. As you declare the truth of God's grace, forgiveness, and empowerment, you increase your own faith. Often, we think of our story of victory as an encouragement for someone else. And, it is. But, as you confess victory in your own life, however small or large, you are reminding yourself of the faithfulness of God and the path of victory you are walking.

A friend of mine used to always yell out, "There's

no I in TEAM!" Sometimes it was funny. Sometimes I just think he wanted me to pass the ball to him. Either way, he was right. Very few, if any, can win on their own. The leprosy of pornography takes a team effort. This washing of confession brings others on your team. You need them. And, quite honestly, they need you. Remember that you are not alone in this. Surrounding you are others who need to benefit from your honesty and your victories.

Who will you talk with? Be specific.

When will you talk with them? Be specific.

How do you think your Initial Confession, Continual Confession, and your Confession of Victory will help others?

BE REAL

WASHING OF
GRACE
WASHING OF
THE WORD
WASHING OF
PRAYER
WASHING
OF ACCESS
WASHING OF
CONFESSION
WASHING OF
TRIGGERS
WASHING OF
ACCOUNTABILITY

HUNGER PANGS

Food is one of God's greatest creations. Well, actually food AND taste buds are a great combination. Now, think about your favorite restaurant. This is the place you drive by, and your car automatically pulls in. When you walk through those doors with an empty stomach, your taste buds know it's time for a party. All of a sudden, the trigger in your stomach demands you order food, and in large quantities. As you look at the menu, everything looks good. The smells then trigger inner sensors, your stomach growls, and saliva glands go into overdrive. It's time to feast.

On the other hand, let's imagine you have just eaten a huge meal. You are stuffed. And, for whatever reason, you have to meet someone at your favorite restaurant. You have a problem. Obviously, you are not hungry. The menu sits in front of you unopened, and eventually you just give it back to the server. There's no need for it. Your stomach and your mind are telling you not to even look at food. You aren't hungry. You aren't ordering. Even the thought of eating one more bite makes you feel slightly sick. What's the difference? When you are hungry, the menu is enticing. When you are full, the menu is almost repulsive.

This chapter is about washing the triggers. A trigger is something that initiates desire and/or a course of action. Now, there are two main types of triggers—internal and external. The **INTERNAL TRIGGER** is the state of mind you most often find yourself in when temptation comes knocking at your door. For many, the trigger to indulge in pornography is boredom.

A 19th century Danish philosopher named Soren Kierkegaard said, "Boredom is the root of all evil."6 Think about that. An idle mind has space for entertaining temptations. More than likely, one of your main internal triggers is boredom. I have also heard that the difference between a good man and a great man is what he does with his free time. Boredom is an opportunity for good or for evil (temptation) to move in.

When your mind and your schedule are empty,

there's room for temptation to be received. On the contrary, if your mind is engaged and there is purpose in your schedule, the trigger of boredom is neutralized.

There are other internal triggers. For some, anger toward others is the trigger which activates a desire to view pornography. Others experience the triggers of loneliness, hurt, bitterness, control, and even entitlement (*I deserve this*).

So, what is YOUR main trigger? What normally precedes the temptation to think about, look at, and watch pornography?

Knowledge positions you for success.

Instead of being blindsided day after day, prayerfully consider the specific internal trigger which precedes your action. A team which knows beforehand which offensive attack is coming is far more prepared to defend against it. Learn yourself. Remember that you control your mind. Your mind should not control you.

However the internal trigger presents itself, recognize it in your life, prepare for it, and diffuse it. This is where the other six washings unite together for victory.

When the internal trigger activates in your life, remind yourself of the transforming, empowering grace of Jesus Christ. Fight out loud with the Word of God. Tune in to the desires of God through prayer. Deny yourself access to the path of pornography. And, communicate honestly about what's going on with someone who is walking alongside you on this journey to freedom. Utilize each of these washings to make the internal trigger ineffective.

Did you know that not only does God want you to diffuse the trigger, but He ALWAYS offers an escape plan for the believer? 1 Corinthians 10:13 says, "The temptations in your life are no different from what others experience. And God is faithful. He will not allow the temptation to be more than you can stand. When you are tempted, **he will show you a way out** so that you can endure" (NLT, emphasis added).

In the darkest moment of temptation, God shines a light on the path of escape. Often, it is a thought: a thought of a Scripture, a clear thought that this choice is not right, a thought to call someone to talk or pray with, a thought to run from the access, or a combination of all of these. The point is that God is more interested in your freedom than even you are. And, He comes through every time with a way of escape. Remember God gives the escape route and the power to take it—every time.

What are the internal triggers you most often experience?

When do these internal triggers usually surface?

What can you do to combat the internal triggers?

BE REAL

WASHING OF
GRACE
WASHING OF
THE WORD
WASHING OF
PRAYER
WASHING
OF ACCESS
WASHING OF
CONFESSION
WASHING OF
TRIGGERS
WASHING OF
ACCOUNTABILITY

RUNNING

A few years ago, I was given a double-barreled shotgun. Up to that point, I had never even fired a shotgun. Wow! That's one loud and powerful gun. Its unique characteristic is that it has two triggers. When one trigger is activated, you absolutely feel it. When both triggers are pulled simultaneously, it's an explosion. As I said in the last chapter, there are two main triggers we deal with—**INTERNAL AND EXTERNAL TRIGGERS.** The internal trigger is a battle in and of itself. But, join it with all of the external triggers, and you have an all out war.

Our world produces external triggers all around us: the pictures on internet devices, the full-body photos at the mall, the revealing clothing worn by those walking by us every day, the commercials, the scenes in movies, and the swimsuits at the pool. The list could go on and on. All of these serve up a platter of external triggers.

Both internal and external triggers are powerful. But, activated together, they can be a lethal explosion.

There was a king named David who decided not to go out into battle. So, what happened to the warring king who sent out his troops and decided to stay home? He got lonely, and bored. One night, David decides to get out of bed and walk around. He just "happened" to walk where he could see a woman taking a bath. Understand, this woman was not his wife, but a wife of another man.

The internal trigger of boredom was colliding with the external trigger of this naked woman. This was not a good combination. James 1 says, "Temptation comes from our own desires, which entice us and drag us away. These desires give birth to sinful actions. And when sin is allowed to grow, it gives birth to death" (14-15, NLT).

This is precisely what David allowed to happen. The internal trigger of boredom remained unwashed and unoccupied by good. The external trigger of this woman remained unwashed. Instead of turning away, he turned toward her. His lustful desire gave birth to sin and sin literally grew to death.

Then, there's the story of Joseph. Here was a young man being pursued by a married woman. The Bible says, "One day he went into the house to attend to his duties, and none of the household servants was inside. She caught him by his cloak and said, 'Come to bed with me!' But he left his cloak in her hand and ran out of the house" (Genesis 39:11-12).

Notice the difference between these two men. One had the internal trigger of boredom firing off. The other was busy attending to his duties. Both had the external trigger of a woman who was available for their viewing pleasure.

One inched closer and closer.

The other ran.

Did you read that last sentence? The other RAN.

The internal and external triggers need a continual washing through prayer, the Word, and running from the temptation.

Check out these trigger washers:

> "Redeem the time, because the days are evil." (Ephesians 5:16)

> "It is God's will that you should be sanctified: that you should avoid sexual immorality;" (1 Thessalonians 4:3)

"Jesus said, 'I must be about my Father's business.'" (Luke 2:49)

"Can a man scoop fire into his lap without his clothes being burned? Can a man walk on hot coals without his feet being scorched? So is he who sleeps with another man's wife; no one who touches her will go unpunished." (Proverbs 6:27-29)

"I have made a covenant with my eyes; why then should I look upon a young woman?" (Job 31:1)

In order for the internal and external triggers to be washed, action much be taken. The Scriptures listed are meant to be lived, not just read. Truly, redeem your time. When boredom strikes, make the most of every opportunity. Passionately pursue the Kingdom of God and His Kingdom purposes for your life. When fatigue increases, carve out time for much needed rest. When feelings of loneliness emerge, pursue friendships with other followers of Jesus. When anger erupts, ask the Lord to help you forgive. Keep the covenant you make with your eyes. An empty mind and life are prime targets for an enemy who wants to derail your life.

Where do the external triggers normally come from in your life?

What differences did you notice in how David and Joseph reacted to the internal and external triggers they faced?

How can you protect yourself from the external triggers?

BE REAL

WASHING OF
GRACE
WASHING OF
THE WORD
WASHING OF
PRAYER
WASHING
OF ACCESS
WASHING OF
CONFESSION
WASHING OF
TRIGGERS
WASHING OF
ACCOUNTABILITY

YOU ARE NOT ALONE

Certain athletes speak of their team going to battle. Sure, it's fun to watch them go head to head for a trophy or a bigger contract. But, sports competitions pale in comparison when you consider real soldiers who go to real wars. It's not a two hour battle where both teams shake hands mid-field after the game. It's life or death. Literally, the life of the soldier beside you depends on you. And, your life depends on him.

What a powerful thought! There are men and women who would actually risk their lives for each other. Their motto is the real deal: *No man left behind, and no one left alone.* Every soldier in the trenches of a battle knows you don't want to be alone. More than that,

You would be insane to think you could make it on your own.

The first part of this washing is **RELATIONAL AC-COUNTABILITY.** The pride in you says you don't need anyone. You can figure out this leprosy of pornography and you can crawl your way out of this hole by yourself. Reality says you are dead wrong. Hear me on this. You weren't meant to be alone. And, in a battle of this magnitude, it's of paramount importance that you are depending on someone else.

Think about the men and women of the Bible. Moses had Aaron, David had Jonathan, Naomi had Ruth, Esther had Mordecai, Shadrach had Meshach and Abednego, Jesus had His disciples, and the disciples were sent out two by two. This pattern is on purpose.

Proverbs 27:17 says, "As iron sharpens iron, so one man sharpens another." This sharpening is more than a one-time conversation. When swords were used in war, they became dented and dulled. This required that they be sharpened again and again. Freedom from this leprosy is not a click of a button. It's a washing. And, this continual, relational accountability with another person plays a vital role in keeping yourself sharp and experiencing complete cleansing.

You must have someone to stand with you during this journey. And, this friend or mentor needs to be someone who will be there over the long haul. Paul the apostle found someone who genuinely cared. His name was Timothy. In Philippians, Paul says of him, "I have no one else like him, who takes a genuine interest in your welfare. For everyone looks out for his own interests, not those of Jesus Christ. But you know that Timothy has proved himself . . ." (Philippians 2:20-22). This person in your life doesn't have to be someone with the same struggle, but they need to be someone who genuinely cares about you finding freedom.

At the core of Relational Accountability is honesty and truth. Essentially, it involves both taking responsibility for your actions and answering for those actions. Because of the personal nature of the struggle, look for someone who is trustworthy and confidential.

The second part of this washing is our own

PERSONAL ACCOUNTABILITY. Every one of us has the ability, if we choose, to keep ourselves accountable. This is accomplished through a consistent, honest evaluation. Here are three questions to help guide you:

What is working?

Think about how the other six washings are helping you. Reflect on healthy thought patterns you have embraced and the triggers you have disarmed with God's strength. Beginning your personal evaluation with the positive reminds you of the forward movement you are truly experiencing.

What is not working?

During the washing of this internal leprosy, you will likely experience bumps along the way. Some days might seem to be easier than the one before. Certain triggers might be easier to wash than others. Honestly assess the moments that have not gone well. This is also the time to take inventory of your access. Often, we have an unrealistically high level of confidence in what we can handle and what we can't. Be honest. What is not working?

What needs to change?

The definition of insanity is to do the same things you've always done while expecting different results. If you do the same things, you will experience the same results. Which of the seven washings have you not set into motion? What needs to be adapted in your fight against this leprosy to propel you forward? Be specific. Take the honest feedback from the first two questions to help you see what needs to change.

One of the fields where we used to play baseball had a restricted area. Although the park containing the baseball fields was large, there was one small fenced in area. As kids, we knew it as an electrical power thingy. More precisely, it was a substation, which housed power transformers. I don't know what genius built it right beside the baseball fields, but nevertheless, there it was. Thankfully, we were old enough to read, and the numerous signs warned of the dangerous high voltage in the fenced area. Even if a ball was hit inside, the signs told us we would be idiots to try to retrieve it. The fence and signs all served as visible restrictions to the potential dangers.

VISIBLE ACCOUNTABILITY is the third part of this washing. Thankfully, there are fences which can place a barrier between you and the leprosy of pornography. Then, even if there is a desire to go into that small restricted area, your warning signs remind you of how dangerous and hazardous that decision will be. Although Visible Accountability through internet filters, restrictions, and tracking reports do not make it impossible to view pornography, they serve as needed "fences" to prevent this internal leprosy from continuing in your life.

Relational Accountability

Do you have someone you can share this journey with? If so, have you openly shared what is going on in your life?

If you do not currently have someone close enough to share this journey of life with, begin praying that God will help you to notice someone who could be that true friend or trusted mentor. List a few people you think you could trust:

BE REAL

BE REAL

Personal Accountability

What is working?

What is not working?

What needs to change?

Visible Accountability

Here are several of many resources to help you have accountability with your visual technology:

Covenant Eyes is an Internet Accountability resource which tracks websites you visit on your computers, smart phones, and tablets, and sends them in an easy-to-read report to someone you trust. This makes it easy to talk about the temptations you face online.

XXXchurch.com offers addiction recovery resources for men, women, parents, and couples. There are weekly articles on how to conquer difficult issues, as well as porn accountability and filtering software.

K9 Web Protection is a free Internet filter and parental control software for internet devices.

Windows Live Family Safety and other freeware provide a simple set of tools for protection from questionable material online. It provides a sense of ease and security with its ability to block and unblock sites and users.

WASHING OF
GRACE
WASHING OF
THE WORD
WASHING OF
PRAYER
WASHING
OF ACCESS
WASHING OF
CONFESSION
WASHING OF
TRIGGERS
WASHING OF
ACCOUNTABILITY

MIND
CHANGE

This journey has been about seven washings: the washings of Grace, the Word, Prayer, Access, Confession, Triggers, and Accountability. Each of the seven washings serve to propel you into freedom. This priceless freedom is possible, attainable, and available for you to experience. However, every one of the seven washings is designed to function as a team with the other washings. Leave one out, and something vital will be missing. It's like a bridge with seven supports.

Remove any one of the supports, and the others are forced to carry more weight.

The result is a weakening of the entire bridge. Do you remember Naaman? Leprosy was destroying his life and his future. Then God stepped in. Then God offered him cleansing. After washing seven times in the Jordan River, his flesh was restored. 2 Kings 5:14 says, "So he went down and dipped himself in the Jordan seven times, as the man of God had told him, and his flesh was restored and became clean like that of a young boy."

Naaman's flesh was restored (refreshed, repaired). The Scripture makes a point to say it wasn't just restored to his pre-leprosy state. Neither was it simply a band-aid which covered the problem.

Naaman experienced a complete restoration of his life.

Naaman's skin was recreated so it was like that of a young boy. This skin was no longer aged, distorted, or worn out in any way. Suddenly his skin appeared as if it wasn't affected at all by years of wear and tear and the effects of leprosy. It was completely renewed.

Do you believe a complete restoration from the leprosy of pornography is even possible? Can the mind be renewed in such a way that the images imprinted long ago or even recently are erased? What would it be like for the places in your mind you have visited so many times to not just be emptied, but cleaned, restored, and repaired?

The New Testament says, "Do not be conformed to this world, but be transformed by the renewing of your mind" (Romans 12:2, NASB). Another translation says, "Don't copy the behavior and customs of this world, but let God transform you into a new person by changing the way you think" (NLT). The mind can be renewed. It's a renovation and an extreme makeover of your mind and actions. Essentially, it is a complete change of your mode of thinking, feelings, and desires.

Through undergoing these washings, you give God the opportunity to reconfigure your mind. The way others are viewed can now be reprogrammed. No longer are others exploited for personal pleasure. Instead, these known and unknown faces can be honored and respected. In addition, your outlook on life will be processed differently. Before, the future looked bleak and healthy relationships seemed unattainable. Now, there is hope and a future.

Try to imagine what was going through Naaman's mind as he journeyed back home. One look at him, and his family and friends would be floored. The story Naaman couldn't wait to share with them would blow them away. He was a changed man! Everything was now different. Even the dreams he had for the future could now be revisited in his heart.

His past was not going to dictate his future.

Now he truly had a future because his leprosy had been washed away.

Can you see down the road to a future that includes a mind reprogrammed and free from your leprosy? The two main roadblocks I see people face as they answer this question are doubt and an unwillingness to fight. First, many people doubt that a complete restoration is even possible. Jesus said, "With man, this is impossible. But, with God, all things are possible" (Matthew 19:26). Why is so much impossible for people? It's because their faith (belief in what is possible through God's power) is not engaged.

As long as Naaman doubted, he was still a leper. But, then he believed and acted on his belief. Then, and only then, Naaman experienced healing. He experienced the impossible become possible through his faith and belief.

The second roadblock many face is the their unwillingness to fight. Sometimes in life a fight is needed. This is most definitely one of those times. Sadly, many are not willing to fight. The easiest thing in the world to do is to continue in the same routine. The road of least resistance is to keep doing what you have been doing.

The restoration of the mind is a God-thing. But, you play a huge role. At what point do you stand up and scream, "Enough"? At what point, do you throw off your jacket, put up your fists, and say, "I will fight for my purity, for myself, my family, and my future?"

Several years ago, I saw a video of a boy being picked on. The bully was having his way with this kid as he had for many weeks. All of a sudden, the kid had enough. No longer would he allow himself to be a punching bag. In that moment, something switched. This boy turned around and gave the bully a beat down. Talk about a surprise. For too long, the enemy of your soul has bullied you. Not anymore. It's time to fight.

It's time to say enough is enough.

The restoration of the mind is possible through these seven continual washings. Believe in what God can do in you. Then fight in His strength for freedom. Ephesians 6:10 says, "Be strong in the Lord and in the strength of His might" (NASB). The unlimited power of God is released through your faith and your fight.

Deep down, what do you truly believe? Is freedom from pornography possible?

In what ways have you begun to taste freedom during this journey?

Are you willing to fight? How will you answer the question each day, "Is it worth it?"

WASHING OF
GRACE
WASHING OF
THE WORD
WASHING OF
PRAYER
WASHING
OF ACCESS
WASHING OF
CONFESSION
WASHING OF
TRIGGERS
WASHING OF
ACCOUNTABILITY

HOPE

Throughout this book, you have likely noticed that these chapters are missing something. There are no detailed descriptions of how pornography destroyed people's lives. Let me explain why. The intention of this book is not to tell you what you already know. Although the leprosy of pornography is extremely destructive and intensifies over time, more than likely, you already know this. Quite possibly, you have experienced it. While it is important to have your eyes wide open to the painful aftermath this leprosy can produce, that was not the purpose of this book. My prayerful intention was for this to be a book of hope, not of fear, a book of victory, not of condemnation. These chapters were not about the effects or the dangers. On the contrary, these were words of escape and freedom.

You very well might have noticed something else missing from this book. It wasn't filled with a story of my battle with pornography. Although I am thankful for those who openly share their past struggles, my story is different. You see, my story in this area is one of God's protection and victory. I can't tell you how many times I have humbly thanked God for guarding my eyes, for godly parents, and for keeping me from stumbling onto that certain website or discovering a discarded magazine.

I do remember one evening as a young kid. Our family had traveled out of state. On this particular night, my Dad handed me the hotel key as the rest of the family was parking and unloading the car. I ran up to the room and entered the empty room. For whatever reason, my first stop was the TV. I started surfing channels. Most likely I was looking for a Celtics vs. Lakers game or an intense gun fight. But, as I flipped through the channels, my eyes saw something my unmarried eyes shouldn't have seen.

The leprosy of pornography doesn't play fair. The enemy will do anything he can to catch our attention and then keep us caught in this downward spiral. So, why am I writing this book? What do I want to say to those battling this leprosy? Victory is POSSIBLE. Victory is ATTAINABLE.

Victory and freedom are AVAILABLE from the Lord by creating the life environment where He can work.

The Scriptures state it is God Himself who, "has saved us and called us to a holy life—not because of anything we have done but because of his own purpose and grace" (2 Timothy 1:8-9). God has created you to live in freedom. And He, through Jesus Christ, has made this possible. Even though you have done absolutely nothing to deserve it, He has chosen to call you to a life filled with His purposes.

No longer is life about you,

but it's all about Him. This promise of freedom is written over your life with the very hand of God.

So go wash yourself—seven times. Like Naaman, this journey will likely be the most difficult one you've ever embarked on. There may be certain washings and certain days that seem impossible. Quite honestly, there might be times when you want to just go back to the way life has been. But, your future will not be dictated by your past. The journey toward freedom is worth going after. This new life in Christ is unlike anything else the world has to offer. The enemy has won for too long. Now, it's time for God to win in your life. Now, it's time for you to win—and truly live free!

NOTES

1 EN-http://www.stanford.edu/group/parasites/
ParaSites2005/Leprosy/history.htm

2 http://www.usatoday.com/story/news/
nation/2013/03/08/surgery-sponges-lost-supplies-patients-
fatal-risk/1969603/

3 Speech by Judith Reisman given at a Science, Technology, and Space Hearing: "The Science Behind Pornography
Addiction," Thursday, November 18, 2004.

4 Ryan Rufus in Living Grace, p. 40

5 http://www.covenanteyes.com/2013/01/07/confess-
porn-secrets-shame/

6 http://www.sorenkierkegaard.nl/artikelen/
Engels/145.%20THE%20ROTATION%20OF%20
CROPS.pdf The Rotation of Crops-page 1

ABOUT THE AUTHOR

Keith Grabill has been involved in youth ministry for the past 20 years, and he has a heart to see people set free. His lifelong desire is to please God and to be the best husband and dad in the world. He is the youth pastor at Christian Celebration Center in Midland, Michigan, where he lives with his wife, Lacei, and their three incredible children.

CONNECT WITH US

We've set up a Seven Times Facebook page. Check it out if you want to connect, tell your story, ask questions, send a personal message, or share Seven Times with people you know. We'd love to hear from you!

www.facebook.com/SEVENTIMES